INDIA

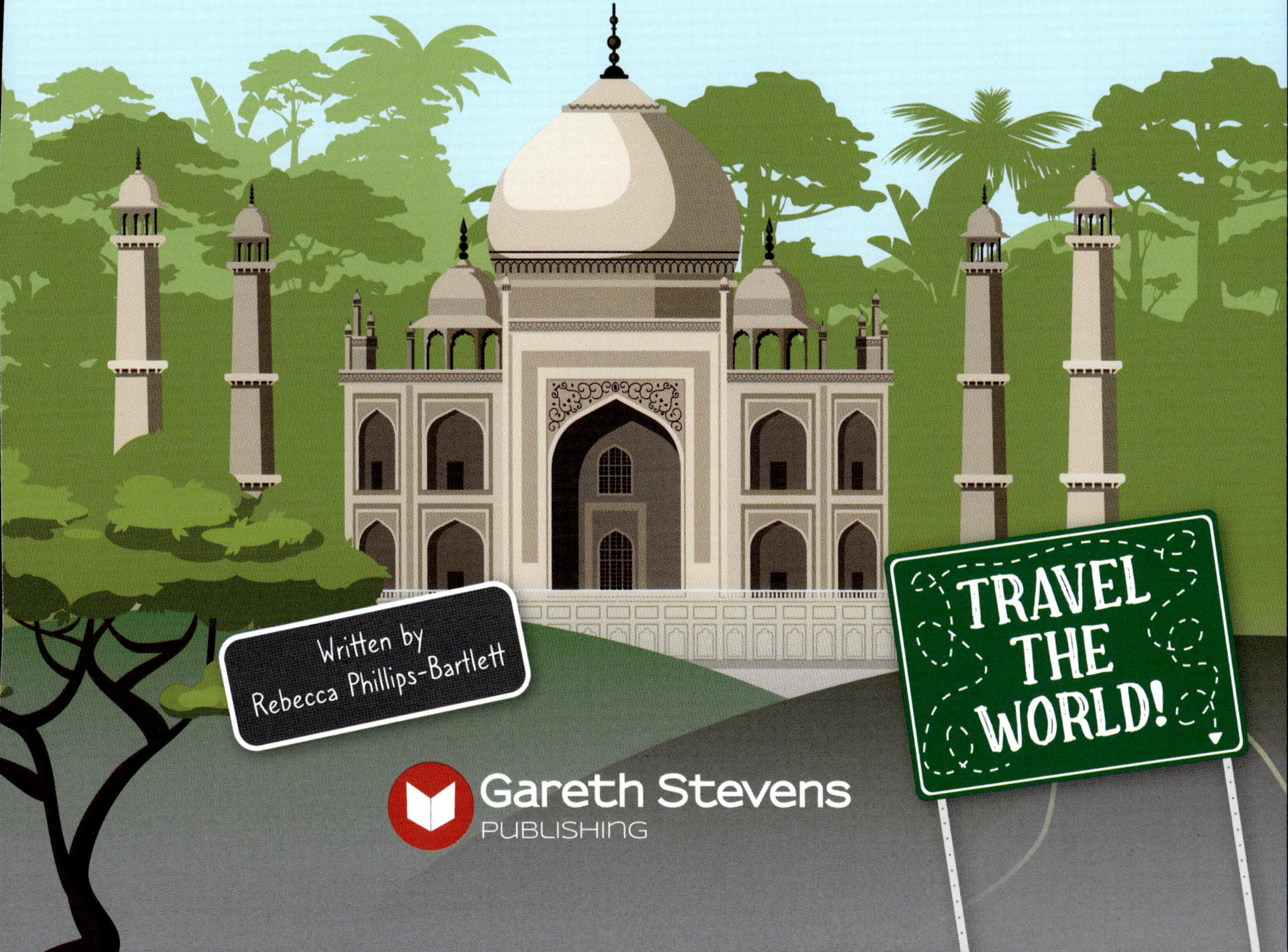

Written by
Rebecca Phillips-Bartlett

TRAVEL THE WORLD!

Gareth Stevens
PUBLISHING

Please visit our website, www.garethstevens.com. For a free color catalog of all our high-quality books, call toll free 1-800-542-2595 or fax 1-877-542-2596.

Cataloging-in-Publication Data

Names: Phillips-Bartlett, Rebecca.
Title: India / Rebecca Phillips-Bartlett.
Description: New York : Gareth Stevens Publishing, 2024. | Series: Travel the world!
Identifiers: ISBN 9781538288368 (pbk.) | ISBN 9781538288375 (library bound) | ISBN 9781538288382 (ebook)
Subjects: LCSH: India--Juvenile literature. | India--Description and travel--Juvenile literature.
Classification: LCC DS407.P455 2024 | DDC 954--dc23

Published in 2024 by
Gareth Stevens Publishing
2544 Clinton St.
Buffalo, NY 14224

Written by: Rebecca Phillips-Bartlett
Edited by: Elise Carraway
Designed by: Drue Rintoul & Isabella Croker

Photo Credits
All images are courtesy of Shutterstock.com, unless otherwise specified. With thanks to Getty Images, Thinkstock Photo and iStockphoto. Recurring images – ONYXprj, GraphicsRF.com, Amitali, WindAwake, artist GSV.. Cover images – Spreadthesign, Sentavio, ANNA_KOVA, Rvector, MuchMania, WindAwake, Nadya_Art, Amanita Silvicora, puputadisaputra. 2–3 – CherylRamalho. 4–5 – Alfmaler, GoodStudio, stockillustration, Vecton, VectorDecor, Stellar_bones, johavel, Kalinin Ilya, creativeline, artist GSV, typoindia by amol. 6–7 – Dr Ajay Kumar Singh, saiko3p, Amitrane, ShustrikS, Tingling1, artist GSV. 8–9 – Redchanka, saiko3p, V.S.Anandhakrishna, Praew stock. 10–11 – saiko3p, imagedb.com, Avigator Fortuner, AlexAnton. 12–13 – stockshoppe, Roop_Dey, Roop_Dey, vinai chunkhajorn. 14–15 – suronin, Lisa Hagan, PACO COMO, GRAPHIC4ART.COM, Macrovector. 16–17 – Mazur Travel, Sarnia, Alfmaler, CRS PHOTO, Akshay AK22, antoniolainezph. 18–19 – Rajesh Narayanan, Noppasin Wongchum, Sun_Shine, CRYSTAL FRAME PHOTOGRAPHY. 20–21 – Dmitry Rukhlenko, riyas.net, Vi design, saiko3p. 22–23 – inithings, QatlasMaps, Mari Dambi.

Printed in the United States of America

CPSIA compliance information: Batch #CSGS24: For further information contact Gareth Stevens at 1-800-542-2595.

CONTENTS

WORDS THAT LOOK LIKE THIS CAN BE FOUND IN THE GLOSSARY ON PAGE 24.

WE ARE GOING ON A TRIP

Hi, I am Deena. We have just packed the car to go on our first road trip. I am really excited to be going on vacation! This year, we are going to India.

Me and Dad

Yesterday, Dad and I looked at this map and planned our journey on it. I am going to follow along on the map while we drive.

SRI HARMANDIR SAHIB

Our first stop in India is Sri Harmandir Sahib. It is also known as the Golden Temple because it is covered in pure gold! This temple is very important for a religion called Sikhism.

THE GOLDEN TEMPLE IS ON A LAKE.

JIM CORBETT NATIONAL PARK

THIS ELEPHANT JOINS US!

OUR CAR HAS TO STOP BECAUSE THERE IS A BENGAL TIGER SITTING IN THE ROAD.

We see lots of amazing animals at Jim Corbett National Park. We go on a safari, which means we drive through the park to see everything.

INDIA GATE

Next, we visit New Delhi. New Delhi is the capital city of India. The first thing we see when we get there is the India Gate. It is over 137 feet (42 m) tall and took 10 years to build!

Me and the India Gate

LOTUS TEMPLE

We visit a temple from the Bahá'í religion. It is called the Lotus Temple. The temple was made to look like a lotus flower. Lotus flowers are an important symbol in some religions.

The Lotus Temple

A lotus flower

Now entering: New Delhi

AGRA FORT

After leaving New Delhi, we visit Agra. First, we go to Agra Fort. It was built in 1573, so it is around 450 years old! Lots of different emperors lived in Agra Fort.

OUTSIDE AGRA FORT

INSIDE AGRA FORT

TAJ MAHAL

The Taj Mahal may be the most famous building in India. It is made of a kind of stone called white marble. The Taj Mahal was built by an emperor as a tomb for his wife.

THE TAJ MAHAL

The art on the ceiling in the Taj Mahal

Now entering: Agra

GANGES RIVER

The Ganges River is a very important river in a religion called Hinduism. It is more than 1,550 miles (2,500 km) long. It travels through lots of very busy parts of India, so it has become quite polluted.

THE GANGES RIVER

VARANASI

Varanasi is one of the cities the Ganges River travels through. Like the river, Varanasi is a very important city in Hinduism.

We go to a market in Varanasi.

VARANASI FROM THE RIVER

KANHA NATIONAL PARK

We go on another safari, this time through Kanha National Park. There are hundreds of different kinds of birds and plants here. Dad and I play a game to see who can spot the most different kinds!

We also see lots of Bengal tigers.

CHAND BAORI

Chand Baori is an ancient stepwell. Stepwells are used to collect water. Lots of stepwells are not used anymore, but Chand Baori is.

Chand Baori is one of the world's biggest stepwells.

Climbing the stairs in Chand Baori

ELLORA CAVES

These caves look a lot more impressive than any caves I have visited before! These caves are human-made. They are full of sculptures from religions such as Buddhism, Hinduism, and Jainism.

Kailasa Temple in the Ellora caves

GOA BEACHES

There are lots of beaches in Goa. We decide to visit Morjim Beach to go turtle spotting. We see lots of olive ridley turtles. The sand on the beach is bright white!

A nest of olive ridley turtles!

MYSORE PALACE

This palace is huge! It is one of the largest palaces in India. When it was first built, it was made of wood. Now, it is made of stone.

WE GO INSIDE THE PALACE.

OOTY

Ooty is a town in the mountains. We ride on Nilgiri Mountain Railway! We also go to see the Kalhatty Waterfalls. The waterfalls are near the jungle, so we try to spot wildlife!

THIS IS THE TRAIN WE GO ON!

KALHATTY WATERFALLS

MEENAKSHI AMMAN TEMPLE

Meenakshi Amman Temple is one of the oldest temples in India. The temple is covered with thousands of sculptures of gods who are important to the Hindu religion.

Meenakshi Amman Temple

KERALA BACKWATERS

We go for a boat ride in Kerala. The boat we go on used to be a boat for carrying rice. Now it is used to give tours.

We ride on a boat like this.

HOME

I had so much fun on our road trip around India. I really enjoyed learning about the different religions and seeing lots of animals. There was so much to do and see!

I would love to go back to India. I would like to visit the Himalayas, which are partly in North India.

I cannot wait to see you.
Love, Deena x

visit India

GLOSSARY

ANCIENT from a long time ago

CAVE a large opening underground in rocks and hills

EMPEROR a ruler of a large area of land, called an empire

GOD a being believed to have more than human powers

POLLUTED made dirty through the actions of humans

RELIGION the belief in and worship of a god or gods

SCULPTURE an object, such as a statue, made through carving or molding

SYMBOL a thing that is used as a sign of something else

TEMPLE a religious building made to give honor to an important figure, or figures, in a religion

TOMB a place people are buried when they die

INDEX